Sonya's suburban house.
A tropical girl at heart.

First published in 2018
by Annointed Daughters Pty Ltd atf the Annointed Daughters Trust.

© Sonya Driver 2018

For stockist enquiries and information, please email hello@thenudge.com.au
or visit www.thenudge.com.au.

ISBN: 978 0 6484168 0 7

THE NUDGE

Written by Sonya Driver

Edited by Kathleen Stephenson

Cover & text designed by Stacey Sherwood

Printed and bound by Inscope Books Australia

Disclaimers

This book reflects the author's present recollections of experiences over time. Some names and identifying details have been changed to protect the privacy of individuals.

First edition

www.thenudge.com.au

 The papers and boards used in this book are from environmentally friendly and sustainable sources.

THE
NUDGE

Claire LIPILE
2023

IMPACT ENTREPRENEURS

Focus: — Health & Wellness

SONYA DRIVER

Trust your gut ♡
Sonya

Sonya's obsession with
bouganvillea.

CONTENTS

DEDICATION

Sorry to be predictable; however, it must be to the
ones that make my heart sing.

My compassionate, beaming daughters Charlotte
and Bronte – much better versions of me.

My Gary, for standing on the sideline and
applauding as I sprint along puffing and swearing.

My lounge buddies – Frankie and Lola (yes,
they're my dogs).

Tan maker up for leader prize

Coast woman behind the develop-
ate Eco Tan range, Sonya Driver, has
ated for the 2013 International Wom-
dership award program.

turned her life around after suffer-
ble blow of a marriage breakdown
's melanoma diagnosis – which both
the same day a few years ago.

ber the day all too well. In a second
exploded into dust," she said.

river managed to get to the point
uld draw inspiration from the diffi-
and went on to develop her own
nic tanning products for men and

and I were both sun lovers and
spray tans after what happened,"

claimed it was a much safer option,
I should have a look into it.
alled at the petrochemicals and syn-
nanufacturers were using to create
products.
p Eco Tan myself."
an range recently made Australian
coming the first and only tanning
fied by the Organic Food Chain

Charlotte Jobson, Bronte Jobson and Sonya Driver, developer of Eco Tan.

under the Australian Government. Judging
the International Women's Leadership A
have commenced and winners will be anno
on March 8.

I rarely sit down. On my afternoon walk I spotted this chair and sat for a moment to breathe. Look for opportunities in your day.

FOREWORD

Those of you that know me will be saying "finally"! I have talked about this manual/book for years. It was already written in my head. I just needed to get it out. Damn, I wish I could telepathically import it to you, but alas I was forced to be focussed and type it. Both, I innately suck at.

So, there are two main reasons I needed to purge this manual from me. Both of those reasons are YOU.

1. To tell my story is to tell the story of millions of Women throughout the ages. To encourage and let them know how incredibly strong and most of all, worthy and valuable they are. If I can rise from the ashes, so can you. I was bullied, discarded, mocked, broke, judged, and best of all UNDERESTIMATED by complete fools!

2. I know it's my calling to mentor people in business. You know how I know this? People ask me all the time. They sense I know. I do. I can walk into a restaurant or any business and my mind makes changes like a computer. I see the blocks and see the invisible success. I usually keep it to myself.

Occasionally, I will open my mouth and I see my husband smirk, like he is mentally saying "here we go". It's always spoken with the intention to lift and help others. I only let rip once the recipient has given their permission for my opinion (which may not be theirs), as most people aren't open to receive the truth or are blocked at change. I love change. Even as I am writing this book; very, very quickly I might add, I'm getting messages and phone calls from people wanting business advice. It's not my profession and I will never charge for it, that way I don't have to censor myself.

So in a nutshell, next time I get asked about mentoring, as I only have 24 hours in a day, I can say "read the manual I wrote".

I give to a myriad of causes and charities, so from each manual, a dollar will go to one of them or a few. My core yearns to help others.

I hope you get something out of this manual that you needed to read. Trust your gut. Tap into it. That is your best business asset. ♥ ♥ ♥

TO YOU I SAY...RISE BEAUTY, RISE.

Sonya xx

I DON'T TRY TO BE LIKED;
I TRY TO KEEP IT REAL,
IT'S NOT YOUR
RESPONSIBILITY TO BE LIKED.

1. A PEEK INSIDE MY STORY

There was a woman named Sonya, that thought she had it all. She was fooling only herself as she shrunk to the role she had to play.

I don't know where that chick is anymore. I hope she is happy, wherever she is, she was so soft and kind. Due to circumstances beyond her control, the soft, kind woman was replaced by a raging rock star (that can't sing), with wings of fire. This crazy bitch rules the roost. I can't tame her. Damn; two health retreats, pilates, yoga (bloody hated it) have tried and failed.

This chick is on fire!

I remember the day; where I sat, the placement of the furniture, what I was wearing, weird shit like that. It was the day my marriage vanished.

Now, I'm not going to go bagging my ex-husband, as the future from this day forward looked after anything I could say but way better. Let's just say, a phone call confirmed what I had already known, he had moved on...

I had taken a redundancy from Qantas as a long haul hostie a few months earlier so I could raise my beautiful girls and become the homemaker of the year! Never did get that damn title or the sash.

OMG, my heart explodes for my girls; their life force is magic. Around the same time, my younger sister Rachael, who had two small girls herself, was diagnosed with a melanoma on her arm.

Now, my sister is the complete opposite to me. She is softly spoken and chilled out to the max. So, it was completely out of character for her to challenge her GP, when he said "no she didn't need a biopsy" on a tiny freckle on her arm, that had changed colour from brown to a scaly red. She went back a couple of weeks later and told her GP she felt something was not right with it and said she wanted a biopsy. That action possibly saved her life. NOTE – SHE TRUSTED HER GUT.

She had what was called "the cut", a deep long scar sits on her arm. The wait to find out if they had it all was a dark time for her and even now she hates talking about it.

So, with the news it hadn't spread, because of her early detection, Rach became super sun paranoid. She lives in an area where the sun blares constantly and even though she wasn't a sun baker like me, she did have fair skin and got burnt easily.

It was around Christmas 2009. Rachael was white as a ghost and said she wanted to get a spray tan. I said "No worries, I will find you a natural one so that it doesn't seep into your scar and blood stream." My beauty therapist told me that hers was 99% natural so I had one, and my gut said "Bullshit, this is all natural!" I asked for the ingredients. I then went home and started researching.

Nature always offers a natural counterpart.

The brand I researched blatantly lied on the bottle. In fact, there were 13 ingredients and only one was natural. It also had FDA warnings and contained many ingredients that were linked to cancer, hormone disrupter's, migraines, seizures and on and on. This brand was the worst at false claims and I have watched their demise over the years and I knew they were reaping what they sowed.

Anyone that has been through a life crisis doesn't sleep well and in my instance, doesn't eat. I lost some weight (I looked hot, haha) not really, a bit too thin for my liking; however I had no appetite. I threw myself into researching and formulating organics. I joined a chemist corner group in the USA and I remember on Christmas Day I called a Jewish chemist with a question about an emulsifier. I only know this because

I apologised for calling him on Christmas day and he said "Don't worry I'm Jewish, I don't celebrate it".

I had bugger all money, in fact I had a tin shed in my backyard where I cut hair for family and friends and made a few dollars. One day my girlfriend came for a haircut and I was in the kitchen mixing solution. She was blown away by my lab equipment (nothing special, bought it on eBay). I can still hear her laughing. She then called me a couple of weeks later and asked if she could invest a little in whatever it was I was doing. The truth is, the money she gave me, I didn't even use for the first two years; however, it was nice to have someone that believed in me when I had nothing but a belly full of fire and desperation.

I was super focussed. I had a lot riding on this. I had to get my tiny house in my name. I needed a loan. I wanted to not rely on anyone for my livelihood or my girls. That was my driving force. If things turned to shit with their Dad (and in the early days it often did) I would be able to pay my share of school fees and no one had control over us or our home.

Yep, the tin shed tha[t]
sat in my backyar[d]
was ECO TA[N]

Laura

School holidays weren't a[s]
they were cracked up to b[e]

With so much at stake I mixed and wrote in my exercise book. I had no bloody idea what I was doing! Research and development was my new hat. I remember shaking in bed one night, as a lady I sold five bottles of my solution to, wanted a refund. It was too sticky, of course it was, I wasn't a chemist and I was trying to work with only organic and natural ingredients. Much, much harder than synthetic ingredients. The colour was spot on straight up though. I would use cacao and grape skin extract instead of toxic food colouring or dyes.

Anyway, as well as making batches of solution, I started sitting in my daughter's bedroom calling potential stockists. Sales, the hardest part of the journey really. Lucky (bullshit, no such thing as luck) for me that's my strength. I love sales. I'm not scared! Most people hate rejection and I suppose I bounce back and shake it off. I always say a mantra in my head that goes like this....

"Ok, so you shot me down now but you'll be back one day."

In the beginning, it was so infuriating because so many beauty therapists believed they were using an organic tan. That's what they had been told by company reps. Guess what? If it has food colouring dyes, it's not organic. Anyway, I did the first bit of sales myself until I hired a happy go lucky neighbour of mine, Carol.

It wasn't long before I got too busy to cope myself, I hired an admin person and then a full-time sales person. All of us were working from my tiny house.

I have an image burnt in my brain of Laura and I sitting in a room, with open bricks as walls and it was freezing. We sat in my fleecy dressing gowns making sales calls. Remember that Laura?

Organically, *Eco Tan* grew and grew. The road was always changing. It was never a straight smooth road. I knew I had to be adaptable and my pace had to remain fast to keep the momentum going.

We moved into a small factory/warehouse and I had started gathering my team. In the beginning, I chose people differently to how I do now. I know what I'm looking for now. We have moved three times and finally I have bought our own warehouse and converted the house on it into an office. I'm so bloody grateful, I know to get to this level it takes many hands. So, my team please take a bow.

People often ask me how I come up with products. Honestly, many different ways; however I'm always looking for a niche. Thinking about what I like to use that I can't find a good one of, is always at the forefront. I believe my products are God inspired.

I do most of my creative thinking in the shower, to be honest. I draw in the fog on the glass and if my instinct goes wild, I know I'm on the right track. Sounds simple. It isn't.

My life now is so incredibly different to eight years ago when I started *Eco Tan*. Completely different.

Top. My original tan solution recipe book I used to formulate my first batch of professional solution.

Right. One of my favourite shots of my team when we were announced BEST GLOBAL ORGANIC BEAUTY BRAND OF 2017

Below. My, how far we've come, ECO TAN early years packaging (so much brown).

PICTURE THE END RESULT
BEFORE YOU TAKE YOUR
FIRST STEP. KEEP YOUR EYE
ON THE GOAL AND JUST
FOLLOW THE ROAD THERE.

♥

I'm now remarried, to a man that is so placid. He never hinders my pace or choices. We rarely talk business. It's funny. He has his own business and I think when we get together we just want to breathe. We NEVER switch off completely.

Honey, if you're reading this, I'm not cutting hair in my shed anymore, so I've cancelled your appointment. You owe me twenty bucks.

Last year Eco Tan/Eco by Sonya Driver won Best Global Organic Beauty Brand of 2017 in the LUX Magazine's Global Excellence Awards based in Europe. I'm so stoked about that. I have travelled to many trade shows around the world, won so many awards for all sorts of our products and have had the absolute privilege to lift others up along the way.

Just recently, I connected with funny lady Celeste Barber (a rare gem) on Instagram. She connected me to Sarah, one of the founders of Rafiki Mwema, a charity that was set up by two incredible mums. One is an

Aussie Mum. In a nutshell, Rafiki is a charity that builds safe houses for sexually abused children in Kenya. Together we raised $100,000 in five days.

To whom much is given, much is expected.

One thing I forgot to mention, when I was in mourning after my marriage ended abruptly, I couldn't shake the grief. I was sick of feeling sad and anxious, so I volunteered for two weeks in East Timor. OMG, helping others that had absolutely nothing, delivered me from the thick fog.

I also went to Romania last year with my GM. I'm actually about to go again this year, while I'm in Europe on business. You see, I heard and saw videos and photos from a friend that travelled there, of a tiny woman and her five daughters living in absolute poverty and despair.

I mean, no door or windows. Romania gets to -15°C and snows. They had; no beds, no water, no toilet, no shower, no food. Just fucken hell.

BE A GIVER! THE MORE YOU
GIVE, THE MORE YOU WILL
RECEIVE IN EVERY WAY! BE
A BLESSING TO OTHERS AND
WATCH WHAT HAPPENS.

I saw a pile of rags with rats living in them and this was where five small girls would sleep. The Mum would dig in the dirt for 13 hours a day looking for worms to sell to the fishermen in exchange for money to survive. I just thought, "this is bullshit, I can do something." *You see we can all do something for someone.*

So, my go getter friend Kerry and I held a lunch at my house and we raised $9,000 to build a bathroom, get water and heating and all the stuff they needed. I visited them before they had water and all the family had was a plastic bucket with a cup in it, filled with dirty water. I just look for opportunities to help. It may be Kenya, Romania, East Timor, Australia; wherever I feel I am called to help, I will.

I want to preach to every woman (or anyone for that matter) out there that no matter how dark your world turns, you are so bloody worthy and valuable. You are enough. You are gifted and stronger than you think. Believe. Push forward. Rise my darling, rise.

Every day we ask ourselves who can we help, whether it's going to Romania to rescue a mother and her children or paying for a dog to have an operation, we get excited by being givers. We have a menagerie of charities, causes and people we lift up, because nothing compares to love.

THERE IS NOTHING TO FEAR

BUT FEAR ITSELF.

DON'T BE AFRAID.

IT'S A TRAP.

DO NOT BE FEARFUL!
IF YOU STUFF UP, JUST MOVE
FORWARD. IT HAPPENS TO
ALL OF US.

2. BRIEF NAG

Buckle up petal... you're ready to roar!

Ok.... So, assuming you have done your SELF checklist (motivation, true calling, prayer, passion, research, BASIC business plan, vision board) you are ready to lay your foundation!

1. Get your domain name first!!!!! NOW!!!!!! Try to get blahblah.com and your country. So, if in Australia you would get the .com.au and the .com. You could go getting every country under the sun. Waste of money in my not so humble opinion. Don't get too paranoid. I have to say, I made the mistake of not getting my domain first and ended up paying $5,000 USD for it. There are companies that wait to buy your product or business domain as they bank on you being a rookie! They got me, the shit heads!

2. Get your social media page handles. The names you want on insta, fb, twitter, pinterest, whatever you are going to use.

3. Remember to search to make sure you are not infringing on anyone's trademark. A costly mistake. I recommend going to a trademark attorney or at the very least putting TM next to the name after you have searched, to make sure no one globally has it. Boring annoying stuff. DO IT ANYWAY.

4. Create an affordable website. DO NOT GET ALL FANCY AND EXPENSIVE! My first website was a free, ugly one. You will naturally upgrade as you go along. Grab a Gen Y and give them $200 bucks to do it. Give them a great brief. KEEP IT SIMPLE.

5. Think logo, font, colours, as this will follow you for your entire life span of the company/product. Keep it simple and don't over think it. Think brand identity. Create a basic style guide. This really means just choosing colours fonts etc. Grab an arty friend to help.

6. Skip this number, I lost my train of thought. Common for someone that has self-diagnosed ADHD. Is this book finished yet? I am in Byron Bay staying with my husband, for the sole purpose of writing this book in two days.... Wish me luck...

7. Do Your vision board, business plan. Now... I swore I would never tell anyone to do a business plan. When I first started I was told by many SMART PEOPLE (insert sarcasm here) to do a business plan. Look... you do have to have some sort of plan. However, do the plan in a way that you will understand it. It's Your vision!

Don't be led down the path by business gurus that don't have a business! That have never actually made it! So many people talk the talk but don't walk the talk! Only take advice from people that have created an empire (no matter how big or small). Look to the doers. Look past the dreamers and talkers. They are still stuck in their dreams. Crave, seek out the doers. They are the dreamers that have stepped out in faith! They are the brave! They hold the key. Yes, the dreamers are really pissed at me by this stage. That's because they haven't yet taken the step. Says more about where they are at than it does about me. Trigger warning for dreamers. X

8. What's your sales channel? Try to come up with more than one channel. I have three.

Example: – selling on your website,

– selling to stores (wholesalers online and instore),

– distributors in other countries!

NEVER HAVE A DISTRIBUTOR IN YOUR OWN COUNTRY!
You are the distributor. Own your back yard.

So many people hate sales and marketing. It is not as hard or scary as you think. It's just connecting to people. Simple. Get out there.

9. A few tips - Insta and facebook, road trips, picking up the phone, least of all by email. I hate doing business by email. I think email should be the last part of a business transaction. It should be to record and reiterate the deal you have going on. It's the minutes.

Throw your super human cape on and get out there. Yes, you will be rejected, that sucks. It is character building. Know that you will be ok. The effort determines the result. Every time you get knocked back, know they will hear from you again in the future. No just means not now!

10. Do the numbers. Ok, I suck at numbers. You can't be great at everything. Work out how much your product costs and then work out the margins. Get someone that is good with Maths to help you. You will have three different margins of profit if you have three sales channels. You get me, or have the two wines I had with lunch taken over this page?

11. Find your tribe. Be consistent, authentic and show your flaws! Get on social media and everyday fight the random troll. Put yourself

out there and your people will come. Be consistent. Be real. Be raw. Be you. We all crave to find someone or something different. In a world of complete BULLSHIT on social media, be real. I look at some of my posts and think I look like shit, what a crap photo. I don't care less. Judge me and it comes back. Love me and it comes back. You need to release the need for approval and giving a damn about what people think of you. Get out there and be strong, just don't be an arsehole about it. ♥

THERE IS NO ONE MORE

TALENTED THAN YOU. THIS

IS YOUR PATH AND LIFE.

ONLY YOU CAN WALK IT.

BE A DOER! DOERS ARE

THE DREAMERS THAT HAVE

HARNESSED THEIR COURAGE

AND STEPPED OUT IN FAITH!

DO THE RESEARCH! BUILD THE
RIGHT FOUNDATION – ASK
YOURSELF; WHY HAVE I BUILD THIS
BUSINESS? WHAT DRIVES ME?
IT CAN'T BE BUILT ON JUST
WANTING TO MAKE MONEY. THERE
HAS TO BE MORE SUBSTANCE.

3. YOUR FOUNDATION

The very first thing you need to settle on is your motivation you have in your heart for the business. Ask yourself, why do you want it so bad? Is it money you're seeking? In my view that won't cut it. The reason why you ask? Money comes and goes and every time you hit a "goes" season your motivation will be a goner. You will always be seeking the allure of money. It's a bloody trap. DO NOT FALL UNDER THE SPELL OF DESIRING MONEY! It has to come from something deeper.

Yes, Oprah is right. Is this your calling? Is it your deep desire and are you good at it? Generally, what you are good at people gravitate towards. People see your talents before you realise them. Even as I am writing this book, I receive a phone call and a message from a woman wanting me to mentor her in business. People sense what your gift is and are attracted to it.

These are questions to ask yourself.

You need to find your calling, mix it with your vision and that will propel you on the right path. If there is no passion or drive, you will burn out and give up when the going gets tough. Believe me, if you're on the right path, the going is going to get REAL tough. Be encouraged by this. In fact, once you get going you will be putting out fires daily.

When I first started, I faced every challenge. If it could go wrong, it did go wrong. Without putting tickets on myself, I don't think most people would have persisted with the crap I went through. There is a saying "An entrepreneur is someone that will spend five years of their life like most people wouldn't, so they can spend the rest of their lives like most people can't."

It takes doing the grind to arrive at the level of success you desire. Even if it's a small level, like a home hair salon, you still need to set the foundations and do the grind to establish it and yourself to be the best in your field. When I do business mentoring, I can quickly tell who I'm going to waste my time on. If they are not prepared to feel the pain and do the grind I will bet their business will dissolve within two years. I see it all the time. We all have those friends that jump on every get rich quick platform out there.

EXAMPLE- The coffee they want to have with you is just to sign you up in their new cult. My senses are so strong to this now, when I smell it I say "You aren't going to try to network market me are you Annie? Because I'm not interested!" Love you Annie! There's nothing wrong with MLM, as long as you're upfront and honest with people. If my being straight offends them, too bad. Their hidden smiling tiger, lurking agenda, offends me!

TIP: THE QUICKER YOU LEARN TO GET BACK UP AND DUST YOURSELF OFF THE BETTER. DON'T TAKE IT PERSONALLY.

SO MANY PEOPLE ARE
TALENTED AND HAVE GREAT
IDEAS BUT SO MANY ARE
PARALYSED BY FEAR! IT
SHOCKS ME – THIS FEAR OF
FAILURE DOESN'T EXIST IT
ONLY EXISTS IF YOU STOP.
I'VE FAILED THOUSANDS OF
TIMES BUT I DON'T STOP.

I DON'T TRY TO BE LIKED;

I TRY TO KEEP IT REAL,

IT'S NOT YOUR

RESPONSIBILITY TO BE LIKED.

LOOK FOR THE KEYS.
KEY PRODUCTS, KEY TEAM
MEMBERS, KEY MARKET,
KEY CLIENTS, DON'T SETTLE.

4. MOVING FORWARD

I don't believe in the saying, forward is forward. It's an excuse! Push forward as fast and as hard as you can. Bash the door down and when you get somewhere and realise it's not going to do you any favours get the hell out! Find another door. Look, it's not who is the smartest or the best, it's actually who can move the fastest.

I know people that are still working on their business plan. People that started their business when I did, still at stage one because they are caught up in getting things perfect.

If you see a niche in the market and take too long to move, someone will also see it and move before you do. It's that simple.

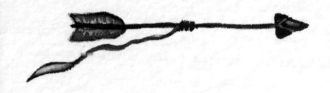

NO, IS SOMETIMES A
HUGE BLESSING AND GET
YOUR SKATES ON. PACE IS
IMPORTANT.

BE AWARE OF THE THING

CALLED FEAR - THE BATTLE

IS IN YOUR HEAD, MOVE

FORWARD ANYWAY.

A GREAT SALES STRUCTURE
IS PARAMOUNT TO ANY
BUSINESS. IF YOU SEE A
THRIVING BUSINESS, THEY
DEFINITELY HAVE A SOLID
SALES STRUCTURE.

5. SALES - SWEET AND SALTY (TEARS)

So many people are terrified of sales. Why? Because it is rejection. Nothing is as rewarding as a customer that said no, then comes back to you at a later date. My sales team thrive on this. If I had my time again, I wouldn't have stressed so much. I would have trusted the process more. No just means, not now.

Selling your wares, ideas and talent will be the hardest part of the journey. You need to dig deep. Surround yourself with the right people. This will be a time that you will feel vulnerable and self-doubt will be your constant shadow. FORGET feeling confident. What a shit liar word that is. I still don't feel confident most of the time. Just fake it. If you're waiting to feel confident before taking a step, you gonna be waiting a long time.

SALES – create more than one sales channel.

If I sold cushions for example.

I would identify what my point of difference is! Why does the world need my cushion?

1. I would start by creating my three sales channels.

2. Sales channel 1 - Online (end users/retail price)
   Sales Channel 2 - Wholesalers (stores and online)
   Sales Channel 3 - International (distributors) = sale

3. I would sell them online on my cheap but classy website = *SALES CHANNEL 1.*

4. I would create a simple catalogue (actually, I would ask a friend to create one for me; same, same) Don't order too much marketing

material as you will change them all the time, and look for cheaper options. You'll need a hard copy and a file to send to wholesale customers via email = *SALES CHANNEL 2.*

5. I would then call every homewares store and send them my pricing and catalogue. I would do a road trip to the stores that want to stock them if possible. *STILL SALES CHANNEL 2.*

6. I would research and contact international homewares distributors = *SALES CHANNEL 3.*

7. I would find and research every relevant expo in my country and attend it (as cheaply as possible).

8. I would be present and consistent on social media every day. I would let my followers see who was behind the brand.

9. As I grew I would hire an admin person as I hate admin/dispatch and it hates me. I know my giftings and that isn't it.

10. What are you really afraid of? The word no? Say no to yourself 100 times until you feel nothing.

Don't go spending money that you don't need to. I'm incredibly generous and incredibly tight. I trust my gut in determining where and what to spend it on. *I would say that has been the greatest asset to me and Eco Tan, my GUT!*

Sales is about consistency. Making contact weekly, monthly or whatever your timeline is. Find your customers, one by one, and train them about your product. Add them to your database (with permission of course) and send out any news specials etc. Don't over do it or they will unsubscribe.

EXAMPLE- I felt like I called every distributor in Australia when I had just three products. Even though I was the only certified organic tanning brand in Australia, at the time no one was interested.

"NEVER HEARD OF IT, we stock an organic tan" (cough cough...BS). I remember feeling so flat and stressed about this. Thank f.... they all turned me down! I sat in my daughter's room and called stores and salons myself and didn't have to cop the small margin of a distributor. I looked fear in the face and head butted it!

TIP - PICK UP THE PHONE! KNOCK ON THE DOOR. CONTACT PEOPLE. KEEP CONTACTING THEM.

PICTURE THE END RESULT
BEFORE YOU TAKE YOUR
FIRST STEP. KEEP YOUR EYE
ON THE GOAL AND JUST
FOLLOW THE ROAD THERE.

FACE REJECTION AND
LEARN TO BE COMFORTABLE
WITH IT. ONCE YOU CAN
SMILE IN ITS FACE, IT ALL
TURNS AROUND.

Lori, mum of 4,
I only use people
in my shoots that I
resonate with. Lori
is a sweet angel .

6. MARKETING MAYHEM

Marketing comes in many forms.

Print media (generally way over priced and doesn't pull the return).

Facebook and social media advertising (if created correctly and analysed daily, this is very effective).

You can also work with influencers on social media to spruik your goods. Try to get people that are like minded and have the same or similar market to you. Example- if I was selling cushions I wouldn't be looking to work with a teenager whose page and audience isn't aligned with mine. Probably isn't your market.

Hustle Heart will set you apart!

♡ You are looking for your fit, the same vibe. We rarely pay people. We do have lots of influencers contact us, and we choose who we work with. I like a positive message. Animal activists and people that stand for something. I see the heart behind people. I would say that's my greatest asset. My ability to read people. I have been called spooky many times in my life, sometimes I know and sense too much.

If your business is a service, can you advertise on your car? If you're a crap driver, I don't suggest it.

Align yourself with other businesses. Go to network, marketing events. Create business cards. Set goals.

Create a media database and write press releases. Send them out. I did this myself and used to get into many magazines and newspapers. I'm a little lazy now and leave it up to my marketing team. *Hustle and heart will set you apart. Remember that.*

Look for opportunities everywhere. Flyers in letter boxes, whatever! Nothing is beneath you! Do the work. Once you have done every part of your business you may pass it to someone else, I give you permission, haha.

Look for charity events you can donate to. It gets your stuff out there plus you are doing a good deed. Win win.

I guess marketing and sales comes naturally to me. I do understand it seems overwhelming though. Write a list and tick it off. Write your story and send it to as many editors you can find. Everything you do has an effect.

Set a six month promotional calendar for your wholesale customers.

Create an email flyer and send it out to your customer database. Both end users and wholesalers.

Enter awards. Know and research your industry. SEE yourself as the leader! Become the authority in your industry.

Have your logo with TM on it everywhere. Think brand awareness.

Most people are visual people, so get a white board on wheels and brain storm.

 You are the best marketer of your business. Connect with people.

EXAMPLE – In my first photo shoot, my girlfriend wore my dress and we borrowed a camera. I made my new boyfriend take photos. Of course, he wasn't a photographer, but he was better than us! Zero budget! I was smart enough to know, don't spend money on a fancy photo shoot! I still think like that! The photos don't remain current for very long. We normally pull them together ourselves. I have outsourced only one, and it was good even with a small budget.

TIP – DON'T WASTE YOUR MONEY ON PRINT MEDIA (THERE ARE ALWAYS EXCEPTIONS). IF YOU ARE GOING TO BUY ADVERTISING IN PRINT MEDIA, ALWAYS NEGOTIATE TO GET A FREE EDITORIAL TOO. NEGOTIATE EVERYTHING. I ONLY SUPPORT A FEW PRINT MEDIA MAGS.

This is from my first photo shoot, my girlfriend wore my dress and we borrowed a camera. I made my new boyfriend take the photos, blurry and out of focus but it'll do.

DON'T BE PARALYSED BY THE
PURSUIT OF PERFECTION!

DON'T BE AFRAID TO
CHANGE SUPPLIERS.
SEEK THE BEST FOR YOUR
BUSINESS

7. SUPPLIERS OF ALL THINGS BIG OR SMALL

Never burn your bridges, unless the bridge is rotten to the core; and then set that sucker alight and run.

My gut tells me when a business relationship turns sour. When I see greed or unfairness I move on. I also call people out on things I don't like, very clearly. That way you are giving people the opportunity to do the right thing. If you still don't feel it's the right fit, move on.

Consider - price, customer service, terms and conditions and the product they are supplying. Tick the boxes off.

It's best not to put all your eggs in one basket. Spread your suppliers out a little.

Terms and conditions. This is the most important part of doing business.

Let me give you an example -

You may get a brochure for 20 cents each from one supplier, cash up front, plus delivery fee. On the other hand, for the same quality and quantity with free delivery, you may get a brochure for 25 cents on a 30 day end of month account. You can pay by Credit Card that earns you points and another 30 days until you need to pay that. Check there are no charges. You get my drift.

Negotiate everything. Don't be scared to create your own terms and conditions. Push the boundaries. I am always fair as I know you need to let other people make money too. Support others and be fair. When you feel it's not serving you or your business, get the hell away from them. *Don't be yoked with shitty people or businesses.*

I only do business with people I like. I don't care about the money.

Reach out to friends and people that can help you in areas that you don't like and aren't your strength.

EXAMPLE - Our freight bill (which is beyond hideous) every year we get quotes again and we always find a better deal or way to cut costs. You may save 50 cents on a parcel with a different supplier multiply that by 800,000 orders per year, you get my drift.

TIP - ASK CURRENT SUPPLIERS FOR A NEW QUOTE YEARLY, AS YOUR BUSINESS GROWS YOUR VOLUME DOES TOO.

DO NOT HOARD.
CLEAN OUT STUFF. MAKE
ROOM FOR NEW DOORS TO
OPEN. FREE YOURSELF.

ASSUMPTION AND

INTERPRETATION ARE YOUR

ENEMY – WRITE IT DOWN.

A STRONG BUSINESS
LEADER KNOWS WHEN
TO SAY SORRY AND ADMIT
WHEN THEY ARE WRONG.
IT'S SO EMPOWERING TO
ACCEPT YOU'RE HUMAN.

8. HOUSEKEEPING

This is annoying, boring stuff that you will want to skip, however, DO NOT. The biggest threat to your business is your lack of attention in this area.

1. The number one creditor is the Australian Tax Office and that also makes them your biggest threat. Don't think you will pay your personal tax later, this is a black hole. I have witnessed this from the outside looking in on a friend in business, who ignored their personal tax bill. I watched in horror as it unfolded. While I was picking carrots, he/she was splashing the cash. Yep, he/she came unstuck. PAY YOUR TAX. DITCH your food delivery app and fancy clothing. Pay your tax and bills. Common sense 101.

2. Get a Fantastic, switched on accountant.

3. Your accounts are everything. Bookkeeping. Get someone that treats your business like it's their own. I have always had a switched on accounts department. You need a money chaser. Someone that will treat your customers with respect, however teach them how to treat you. If you are a pushover, no one will pay their bills on time. My customers know Eco Tan are by the book. Teach people how to treat you. I have even had a past accounts lady knock on the door of someone that owed us money. I didn't know about this until after the fact and I don't think it's entirely legal. Oops.

4. Contracts - read them carefully. Get a lawyer friend (haha) it will save you heaps. Read and change everything. You know more than you think.

5. Check your trademarks. Get assistance on this.

6. Don't be scared. It's not who is smartest that wins. It's who has the most determination and persistence that does.

7. Check terms and conditions on everything. Change them. DO NOT BE AFRAID. Make your own terms.

AT THE END OF THE DAY,

THE EFFORT

DETERMINES THE RESULT.

I DON'T FOCUS ON THE
NEGATIVE OR TOXIC PEOPLE.
IF THERE IS SOMETHING I
NEED TO LOOK AT IN MYSELF
I WILL, I'M ALL ABOUT SELF-
DEVELOPMENT BUT I DON'T LET
PEOPLE DESTROY ME. I DON'T
ENGAGE THEM AND I KEEP
MOVING FORWARD.

9. CUSTOMER SERVICE

Firstly know who your customers are. The public and the stores that stock your product for instance.

The one thing my staff know about me is that every customer needs replying to asap. They all know that's my number one! I don't care if it's only a $20 purchase. They are just as important as a $100,000 order.

I will often get on our social media and end up counselling someone who was initially abusive for whatever reason. I will get a text from Anna saying 'your friend needs you in the DM's'. They all hate it when I jump on as I talk to everyone like they are my daughter or bestie. I hi-jack the page. I also do everything fast and never check my spelling or grammar so the messages are a puzzle in themselves. No apologies here, people feel the love. I never want to be insta-famous personally, as I couldn't sleep until everyone got a reply. I'm a rookie! The bloody wine has taken me down a rabbit hole.

1. Always respond asap to ALL customers.

2. Hear them out. Is there merit in what they are saying?

3. Do you need to apologise? Only the strong can master this. It's a brilliant business act as it diffuses any situation.

4. Do you need to refund them and let them go?

5. Know when to cut them loose. There will always be difficult customers, that no matter what you do they complain and are never happy. THAT'S BECAUSE THEY ARE NEVER HAPPY. You need to know when to cut them loose. Bless them and release them. Your time is burning away with someone that really just wants to fight.

6. Remember 80% of your business comes from 20% off your customers. That doesn't mean treat them any different. It just identifies who are the ones that need more encouragement, training and who are the ones that you need you to create new promotions, marketing, for example. If they are pushing forward with your product, support them!

7. Always put yourself in their shoes. There is always two sides to every story, so make sure you gather your facts.

8. Have a service recovery policy in place. If you stuff an order up, pay the freight and do what you have to do to make it right.

TO BE HONEST, SOMETIMES THE CUSTOMER ISN'T RIGHT, HOWEVER EVERY CUSTOMER HAS THE RIGHT TO BE HEARD, VALUED AND RESPECTED.

EXAMPLE - We have a store outside of Australia that doesn't like their rep. They even changed their name, as they had a fight with the franchisees. They complain if they pay freight, fight over paying their bills, on and on and on. I have watched this store for years. The owner has the darkest energy and I'm sorry to say, their staff have the same vibe and guess what? So do their customers. Miserable and moody! In case you are wondering, they are far from flourishing.

TIP – DON'T BRING YOUR DARKNESS INTO YOUR BUSINESS. BRING IT TO LIGHT. GO SEE A PROFESSIONAL. IT COMES DOWN FROM THE TOP. YOUR VIBE SPREADS AND WILL TOTALLY AFFECT YOUR BUSINESS OUTCOME.

This is my favourite tree; the pandanus. It's on the beach at Currumbin... I stop here and take a photo almost every day on my walk.

10. H-Ahhhhhhhh OR HUMAN RESOURCES

You can't ignore an area of your business because you don't like it; Say tax. If you don't like something find someone who does and hire them to do it. Gather smart, driven, exceptional people around you. When I'm gathering my tribe, I not only look at their strengths, I really focus on their weaknesses. We all have them. If you can pinpoint a weakness you can work on it! I call it poking the egg. I'm looking for the weak spot of the egg and I need to ask myself if I can live with it?

It hurts me badly when I have to cut people loose, because I fall in love with them. I see their potential, even if they can't.

So, in other words, don't hire people just because you like them. I have to wear a different hat when hiring. I get it right most of the time.

When I don't, they have to go. Leaving the wrong person in a position is a disaster. It won't do them any favours or anyone else.

Read what they aren't telling you. Call references. If they job hop or talk bad about their last employer, guess what? Chances are they will be doing it to you also. You shall know them by their fruit.

THE BEST PART ABOUT BUSINESS IS PEOPLE. THE WORST PART ABOUT BUSINESS IS PEOPLE.

Always have a probation period in writing. Clearly have your expectations and job description written down and always have 'not limited to' on it. In other words, the role may change to some degree.

I hire on character. Attitude, the fire I sense in them. I can teach the rest. If they are dynamic enough they will research and find a way. I basically teach myself everything. I still suck at technology because I don't like it. Funny thing is my Mum thinks I'm a guru at it. My kids have to program Netflix for me. I suck at it.

Be straight with people, and in turn, ask people to be straight with you.

In my team, I can tell you what I think motivates them. They are all different. The thing I'm very proud of is when outsiders come to visit our office, they always comment on the vibe of the place and the people. Happiness runs deep. Not every day but most days, we all have each other's back.

Every department, big or small needs its own manual. Just bullet points of key areas; Structure, policies and procedures.

Number it!
Don't overdo it.

So, if someone was sick that day, a new person could come in and pick up the simple manual and take over.

I HAVE CREATED MY OWN
PROCEDURE CODES FOR MY
COMPANY.

CODE RED
Do it immediately

CODE ORANGE
Needs to be done by the end of
the business day

CODE GREEN
Needs to be done before the end
of the business week

YES, YOU CAN USE THIS.
MY PLEASURE.

A.B.C.R.

A - Allocate/assign a
person to a task

B - Brief them on the task

C - Closing time. When the task
needs to be completed by

R - Report back on the task
given once finished

Be quick to jump on any negativity. It spreads like an insidious weed. Always have two people talking and making notes when dealing with issues.

In the beginning, I paid my staff more than myself. It wasn't until I was personally struggling that my accountant said to me, you need to pay yourself more! When you start out, you most likely won't have an abundance of funds to spread around. I knew to make my business grow how I wanted it, I would need to put myself last. I had a very simple lifestyle. Still do. I always pay well above the award and often buy flowers and gifts for my team.

Actually, I have even given my car to one of my team that didn't have one. Bonuses, massages monthly, lucky dips, a day off, whatever it takes to let that person know how appreciated they are and valued. I'm sure not everyone will like me, and guess what you can't give a rats arse if they do or not. Seriously, be good to everyone and it's their choice if they like you or not. It's none of my business. Having said that, I am tough. My expectations are high. I hate BS and bad attitudes and will not put up with it. My staff often say they love me and they say they are a little bit scared of me too. Haha, wish my kids were.

Make sure your team are being heard. I can't stand whingers that don't speak up and then complain and play the victim. So, we always ask if anyone has any ideas or feedback. Have a communications book too. Be happy to listen. Some things you will take on and other things you won't. Brain storming is fabulous for creating a higher energy and united team.

Check all the legal requirements for employing people in your area. Know the facts! Not as hard as you think. Nothing is hard really. It just takes research and doing the work.

WE NEVER HIRE ON
QUALIFICATIONS ALONE.
WE LOOK FOR CHARACTER
AND ATTITUDE; THE REST
CAN BE TAUGHT.

EXAMPLE - In the early days, a great dynamic, smart, young guy came to work for me. What I knew was that his down side was he was a party animal! I hired him anyway. Of course, he was unreliable and let us down too many times by not turning up to work. Which in turn put extra stress on everyone else. We still love him but he had to go.

TIP- AFTER MEETINGS ALWAYS DO QUICK MINUTES IN WRITING SO EVERYONE IS ON THE SAME PAGE. ASSUMPTION AND INTERPRETATION ARE THE ENEMY.

THE TRUTH IS

ALWAYS VISIBLE.

LOOK DEEPER.

I'VE FOUND ALONG MY
JOURNEY THAT PEOPLE
WITH DRIVE RARELY HAVE
EXCUSES, AND THOSE
WITH EXCUSES RARELY
HAVE DRIVE.

I took this photo on a day when I needed an angel and I was sent one... or many.

11. HELLO JUDAS

(SAID IN A LOW MONOTONE VOICE)

Just hang on a tick while I get a glass of wine. This will be a painful trigger page, so grab yourself a cuppa or vino too.

Ready??

Well hello Judas... you jealous coward, with no brains. (I thought I would start softly...)

Who is your Judas? It's those you keep super close to you. The ones that you THINK have your back, front and heart. The ones you invest your time and love in, then they stab you in the face. A few people spring to mind, do they?

Only a Judas can truly hurt you. Like a husband running off with another woman or your best friend siding with an enemy, stuff like that. Beware the Judas. They are your inner circle. Now don't get all paranoid and be a negative nelly. Just be aware of not giving too much info, love, money, power or most importantly too much of yourself.

They are the smiling tigers, the polite ones, the nice ones. I trust crazy friends over any controlled, pleasant peep. Why the hell are they so civilised? Because they are hiding who they are!

Ok, the two sips of wine have opened a weird door in my brain so let's walk through it shall we? The moral to this rant is NEVER 100% trust anyone! Never ever.

Betrayal is such a painful wound. This is what I know!

I have witnessed it over and over. They all come undone! I have had a handful of Judases in my life, both professionally and privately.

ALWAYS BE STRAIGHT WITH
PEOPLE. NO ONE LIKES A
SMILING TIGER. YOU MAY
LOSE SOME PEOPLE BUT
THE ONES WHO STAY WILL
ALWAYS HAVE YOUR BACK.

I have watched in awe them reap what they sowed. I have never taken up revenge or wished bad on them, in fact, as I know there is a higher power, I relax in the spiritual process of sowing and reaping (some call it karma). Know that the higher and more successful you become, your circle gets smaller as the humans around you show their cracks... Jealousy is a big one.

"Too big for your boots, who does she think she is?" My favourite one is "She's not that smart, I can do better". They are wrong on so many levels. As my friend Angela says "You, Sonya are an innovator not an imitator".

EXAMPLE - I have had people I have trained, rescued, believed in, placed in positions of power, even though I knew they weren't capable of the role, betray me beautifully. Everyone knew it and I knew it. I would just do their job too. I have had Judases steal my name, my story, my database and more. I have also watched them fry in my wings of righteous fire!

TIP: WANT TO KNOW WHO YOUR JUDASES ARE? PRAY TO GOD AS YOU FALL ASLEEP TO SHOW YOU, OR TRUST YOUR GUT. WAKE UP WITH A SENSE AND THEN WATCH THE REVEALING PROCESS UNFOLD. GRAB THE POPCORN.

BE SURE TO TAKE BREAKS TO REFOCUS. IT'S A GREAT WAY TO MOVE FORWARD WITH MORE ENERGY AND FRESH EYES.

12. BACK THY SELF

So you're an imposter...

Join the club. Really, who has all the answers? Only Bullshit artists.
Just use your gut feeling and do everything with a good heart and keep
moving forward. Do not lie!! It all comes back. I don't actually care if
you believe that or not. It's a fact. Everything you do has a consequence.

I mean I was a dumped single mum with shit all money and I created
a global multi-million dollar company from using my GUT instinct. I
failed daily. I got straight back up. No one has travelled your road or
started your business. Only you. Only You.

If I stuffed up I always apologise or own it. I never play the victim. Only the strong can admit they are wrong.

I have drive and determination, that's the battle. If you are looking for some fast track or manual on making it. Sorry, this ain't it. Just keep moving forward, own your mistakes, forgive yourself and others and move forward. You are not going to know everything about your new venture. Of course, you bloody don't. I still don't. The difference is, now I trust my gut instinct and I'm 95% right. Sounds arrogant, I know. Every time I second guessed myself or didn't tap into my gut I regretted it. You are the success behind you.

BACK THYSELF.

EXAMPLE- I could give you hundreds of examples when I didn't think I could possibly know the answer. Here is a MAJOR ONE.

So, one our online global sales channels had dropped by 67% one month... WTF I quickly hired an in house brilliant geek, a team of new experts and had my management team looking into it. They came with loads of lingo and explanations; however, I knew collectively they were all wrong.

I went online myself and within five minutes I had the answer and shot down a circle of mega stars and apparent geniuses. The trouble was, it was a maze to actually make a purchase. It needed simplifying. Easy! You know more than you think! That was a huge lesson to me. I have common sense and if I created a global pioneering company there must be something that God has instilled and trusts me with.

TIP- IT'S SELF-BELIEF THAT YOU WILL BE OK REGARDLESS. IF YOU DON'T HAVE IT. FAKE IT. ONLY THE BRAVE WILL MAKE IT. NOT THE SMART. NOT THE RICH. THE BRAVE!

THERE IS A SPIRITUAL LAW
AT WORK – IT'S CALLED
REAP AND SOW. IT'S SO
IMPORTANT TO UNDERSTAND
WHAT SEASON YOU'RE IN.

AVOID TOXIC PEOPLE LIKE
THE PLAGUE. IF SOMEONE
DOES NOT MAKE YOU FEEL
GOOD, THAT IS YOUR GUT
TELLING YOU TO RUN.

13. COMPETITORS AND IMITATORS

Now, most people watch their competitors. I never ever have. Simply because I have my own ideas and don't want to be taken off track. Also, it will piss me off if I see BS so I just stick to myself. I look to be a leader not a copycat.

I don't buy copycat brands either. I support the originals.

So, if you're forging ahead with your own ideas, you don't need to look. I don't spend my energy on things that don't bring a positive return. Many in business will disagree with me and that's OK. I have also seen people that are obsessed with competitors, stalk them and then get angry. It stops them from moving forward. I just smile and say, "well I'm going to beat them in the market". I never pick a fight; however, I defend like a psycho bitch from Mars. I bring the battle to new levels. Spiritually and worldly.

EXAMPLE - I remember when I was making my solution from my house and I put my twenty clients on my website and I mistakenly added their address and phone number. A horrible (no seriously, they are) synthetic tanning company sent every one of them two litres of their toxic solution and other freebies. It would have crippled me financially, however my clients were the ones that knew organic ingredients and were repulsed by the cheap, toxic garbage they were sent. They all contacted me too. I so appreciated the loyalty, it's rare these days. There are dirty players out there. My mind was pure (ish) then, now it's suss with squinted eyes.

TIP- IF YOU ARE AN INNOVATOR YOU WON'T BE COPYING OTHERS, SO DON'T WORRY. YOU WILL BE AHEAD AND SAILING YOUR OWN BOAT. MAKE IT HARD FOR PEOPLE TO CONTACT YOUR CLIENTS. SECURITY!

FOCUS ON YOUR
OWN BUSINESS. NOT
OTHER PEOPLES.

BE ETHICAL. CHECK
YOUR MOTIVATION. DO
EVERYTHING WITH A GOOD
HEART. IT ALL COMES BACK.

YOUR VIBE ATTRACTS
YOUR TRIBE. YOUR TRIBE
DETERMINES YOUR VIBE!

EVERY DAY IF YOU'RE
FORGING FORWARD IN
BUSINESS, YOU WILL BE
PUTTING OUT FIRES. TAKE
THIS AS A GOOD SIGN. NOT
ONCE HAVE I SAT RELAXING
BEHIND MY DESK WITH A
BUNCH OF FLOWERS.

GET AS MANY VALUED
ACCREDITATIONS AS YOU
CAN. IT SENDS A STRONG
MESSAGE ABOUT THE
AUTHENTICITY OF YOUR
BUSINESS.

14. SELF MANAGEMENT

Now, for many years I didn't think I was worthy to call myself an entrepreneur. Then I started coming across articles about other entrepreneurs and I realised, shit, that's what I am. It gave me peace of mind to have this label. I used to beat myself up, as I wasn't like most business people I met, I sucked at some areas and I had made the mistake of believing I should be great at all areas.

I didn't have a desk, I worked from my phone, still do. I rarely sleep. I don't have an office. I don't like holidays. I hate massages and relaxing. I'm always pushing everyone around me forward and have had two bouts of glandular fever I didn't even know about, according to my Doctor. I just surge on. I'm always seeking to help others with their problems. I don't socialise or do networking events (not saying you shouldn't).

WHAT YOU THINK OF ME
IS NONE OF MY BUSINESS
& WHAT I THINK OF YOU IS
NONE OF YOURS.

I decline most public speaking invites, purely because I find it hard to stay on track. The small amount of public speaking that I have accepted have apparently been unforgettable. I have had letters from leaders afterwards saying thank you for tapping into what I needed to hear. I don't know if my speech was amazing or the swearing had them in shock.

I hate the word professional. I have never been professional in my life. It's just another mask I have to break through. I'd rather go into meetings UNPROFESSIONAL and be straight up. Let them judge you. I don't care.

Does any of this sound like you? Give yourself and others a break.

One of the hardest things for people to do is delegate. Seriously, they think they can do it better and in most cases they can. That's not the point, the point is to get it done. Forget perfection. It doesn't exist.

See your work load as a spinning plate and the rule is keep it moving, stuff coming on and stuff going off. It's in the pace. Use ABCR and get it off your plate.

So, what I tend to do is, I will have a week's get away. Not for me! For my team, to let them catch up. I can't go for two weeks or I think they will fall into an admin trap (they won't because they are all amazing and I'm probably annoying them via email anyway). I need to remove myself so they can catch up and we all can recharge.

So, mentally I'm incredibly strong. I'm so grateful for that. Find what recharges you. Identifying what doesn't, is a start.

I love to walk in nature, Netflix, find a great series, an occasional fine dining experience (not too much as I hate wearing bras). I ask God daily to restore me, bring me newness, carry my burdens and silly worries. (Yes, I'm a Jesus freak).

Now that's me, you do what you know is kind to you. Remember, it all flows down from the top. Just like lava.

TIPS- find the things that recharge you. ⭐ ♡

I walk.

Hang with the people that don't drain you.

Listen to music.

Take long baths. (because you can't have your phone on as you will get electrocuted)

Juice on. (not bong on)

Health - example. If you hate the gym don't go! Find something you enjoy, that gets you moving. Join a hiker's group, running club. Find your community. Have fun.

Laughter.

Tap into your creative side occasionally.

Plan something to look forward to.

EXAMPLE - I know I distract my team with new ideas and projects and my speed is super fast. I get so frustrated by 'normal pace', so on Wednesday's I work from home and have created a LOCK DOWN structure. So my team are in lock down. No distractions. The admin trap is always going to be there. So creating lock down for anyone that needs it, stops excuses and gets shit done!

TIP - GO GET OUTSIDE, DETACH FROM YOUR PHONE ON WEEKENDS. CHUCK A BLANKET ON THE GROUND, EAT DRINK, SLEEP.

WHEN PEOPLE ARE
IMPEDING YOUR SUCCESS
IN BUSINESS OR LIFE, THEY
HAVE TO GO. BE KIND
RELEASE THEM TO THEIR
CALLING.

DON'T BELIEVE THE DARK
THOUGHTS YOU TELL
YOURSELF. ESPECIALLY LATE AT
NIGHT. YOU ARE WORTHY AND
SMART. NO ONE CAN TAKE
YOUR PLACE ON EARTH.

15. REFLECTIONS
FROM MY SEE-THROUGH VAULT

Don't trust anyone 100%.

Don't beat yourself up.

Don't be a copycat.

Be ethical and don't be a Bullshit artist.

Be a giver.

Don't listen to talkers learn from the doers.

Check terms and conditions on everything.

No one is smarter than you... seriously they are not.

Security.

Put everything in writing.

Push and nag - the squeaky wheel gets the oil.

Trust your gut!!!

Trust your gut!!!

Fight against stress daily.

You can't skip the grind – do the work.

Don't be stuck in the 'striving for perfection' rut.

Know your strengths and weakness.

Say sorry and move on.

Collect people that feel like sunshine not rain

PRAY! X

DON'T UNDERESTIMATE

THE POWER OF PRAYER.

SAIL YOUR OWN COURSE.
DON'T COMPARE YOURSELF
TO YOUR COMPETITION.
BE UNIQUE!
BE AN INNOVATOR NOT
AN IMITATOR.

CRAVE THE PEOPLE

THAT FEEL LIKE SUNSHINE.

BAKE IN THEM.

THANK YOU

Thank you to my LOW MAINTENANCE husband Gary. Thank you to my Mum, who is without a doubt the kindest human I've ever met (& for minding my dogs). My team; Mish (earthly angel), Kelly, my rock Mitzi. My hedgewoman Lisa, my pavement buddy Stacey, our pocket-rocket Alli. Laura, who has been with me on every rollercoaster I ride. She is one of my people that I call when I (rarely) struggle to get back up. Everyone that came for part of the way or all of the way on this journey with me. Thank you. My apologies if I was a cranky bitch, you know I love you.

My brother Paul. My Sister Rachael, who is wise beyond this realm. If she speaks, write it down! The funny thing is she thinks she is dumb. The irony!

Everyone that has been a part of Eco Tan from the beginning, Thank you. I started writing a list of names; however I couldn't sleep as I was worried I forgot someone. So I honour and sincerely thank you all, even if you were a shit to me; thanks.

My Indian family; that tell me they love and appreciate me all the time and bring me amazing food. Rimmy and Joe, Raveen. Take a bow. My two daughters; Charlotte and Bronte. They were the absolute core of pushing myself to manifest and create this company. You both have seen, heard and witnessed the struggle and pain. I always tried to think of you first, your childhood, your feelings, sorry for always being on the phone or working. Whatever I need to say sorry for.... SORRY!!!!!!

Without the need to provide you with a strong role model as a mother and a woman, I most probably would be sitting in a campervan listening to Fleetwood Mac somewhere around Byron. Shit, that sounds so good.

My copycats, trolls, haters and scammers. Thank you for showing me your darkness, that made me really value my light.

The last thing I want to leave you with is this -

EVERYTHING WILL BE ALRIGHT, PROMISE x